VISION QUEST

A VISUAL JOURNEY THROUGH NORTH CAROLINA'S
LOWER ROANOKE RIVER BASIN

PHOTOGRAPHY AND TEXT BY CARL V. GALIE JR.
INTRODUCTION BY J. MERRILL LYNCH

RED MAPLE PRESS

© Carl V. Galie Jr. 1998

Red Maple Press
PO Box 20143
Winston-Salem, NC 27120

Roanoke River Map designed by Sue Meyer
Poem: "Wouldn't It Be Great If" written by Nick Greco © 1998

ISBN 0-9669876-0-8

Library of Congress Catalogue Card Number: 98-068597

Printed in China by Everbest Printing

First Edition

Acknowledgments

So many have contributed to this project in every conceivable way that listing them all would be impossible. I only hope that those I may have unintentionally forgotten will be understanding.

I would first like to thank the Winston-Salem/Forsyth County Arts Council and the North Carolina Arts Council for their support in the form of the emerging artist grant.

I would especially like to thank J. Merrill Lynch, The Nature Conservancy – North Carolina Chapter associate director of protection, for agreeing to write the introduction. Growing up on a farm near the Roanoke, Merrill spent his childhood exploring its banks. He was also the scientist who spent four years surveying the 137-mile lower Roanoke River Basin and determined that it had the largest intact and least disturbed bottomland hardwood and cypress-tupelo ecosystem on the Atlantic Coast. Merrill's love and understanding of the region is obvious in his introduction.

Thanks to Nick Greco and his parents, Ann and Michael, for granting me permission to use Nick's poem. The seeds of thought that we plant in our children when they are young will someday take root. May we all be wise gardeners.

I don't even know how to begin thanking Gail and Riley Roberson. They opened their home to me, a total stranger, and made me feel like one of the family. Now Gail and Riley have become two of my dearest friends. Gail, an award-winning author and columnist, became my unofficial editor. She introduced me to so many people that it is impossible to name them all. Ricky Legget, Doug Abernathy, Henry Winslow, Jeff Snell, and Jerry Hardison are just a few of the many who shared with me some of their favorite spots along the river. In my heart I know this book would be nowhere near completion if it weren't for Gail and Riley's help and encouragement.

I would like to thank Jeff Horton, the Roanoke River Coordinator, and the staff of The Nature Conservancy – North Carolina Chapter for their help over the last four years. I would also like to thank Jamey Gerlaugh and the Roanoke River Partners for their continued support of my photography.

Special thanks are in order to Frank Lawson, president and owner of Prepress-Graphics Inc., for giving me access to all the resources of his company. His generous gesture was probably the determining factor in making the decision to form my own company to publish this book. Having access to Prepress-Graphics' talented staff for everything from scanning the images to proofing the final draft has made this a much easier task. If there is any criticism in order for this book, it is due to my stubbornness and not taking all their advice. Thank you, John Mason, Cindy Davis, Jim Mabe, Stephany Ellingham, Debbie Mathis, Tim Tuttle, Audene Church, and Gray Renegar, for all your input on this project.

Finally I would like to give thanks to my Creator, for opening my eyes and my heart to the many wonders of this world. I only hope that these images have done them justice.

Introduction

The Roanoke River floodplain is very special to anyone who has been lucky enough to experience it. The Roanoke is one of the great brownwater rivers of the southeastern United States. Rising high in the Ridge and Valley province of the Southern Appalachian Mountains of western Virginia, the river flows more than 400 miles to the southeast where it empties into North Carolina's Albemarle Sound. Going from north to south, the Roanoke shares company with four other major rivers which drain the eastern slopes of the Southern Appalachians: the Yadkin-Pee Dee, the Catawba-Santee, the Savannah, and the Altamaha.

These great rivers are similar in that they all originate in the southern Appalachians and are classified as alluvial or brownwater rivers. Fed by surface runoff, they pick up speed, and volume, as they flow to the sea. Each has a huge catchment basin consisting of thousands of secondary rivers, streams, and creeks that catch the surface runoff of water and sediment. At the fall line, where the rivers flow from the crystalline rocks of the Piedmont into the flat, sedimentary deposits of the Coastal Plain, the rivers have deposited huge amounts of sediment, forming wide, deeply forested floodplains with bottomland hardwoods adapted to periodic flooding. This bottomland hardwood ecosystem actually contains a number of different vegetation zones, each of which is adapted to different degrees of flooding. The classic cypress-gum swamp forest, often characterized by trees festooned with Spanish moss, is one of the dominant vegetation types in this bottomland ecosystem.

The Roanoke River can be characterized as having three distinct personalities. At its headwaters in the Virginia mountains, the river is relatively small and flows through a beautiful rural landscape alternating between farmland, pasture, and mountain gorges. The river drops out of the mountains near Roanoke, Virginia, and enters the rolling hills of the Piedmont. Here the river's character has been greatly altered by the industrial hand of modern civilization. Once a large river flowing through rich farmland, extensive forest, and human settlements, the river is now mostly drowned beneath a series of hydroelectric reservoirs: Smith Mountain, Leesville, Kerr, Gaston, and Roanoke Rapids. These reservoirs have temporarily drowned the flowing river still flowing silently underneath the cacophony of ski boats and jetskis. Farther downstream, the river drops over its final rapids at the fall line. Here, along the final 137 miles of the river's journey to the estuary of Albermarle Sound, the wild character of the river and its floodplain has remained relatively unscathed.

Probably the best way to fully experience the Roanoke River is to spend the night alone there in the spring. It may sound antisocial, but having another person around can be distracting. If you are lucky you'll soon forget about yourself and start focusing on the environment into which you've voluntarily ventured.

More than likely you will soon be reminded that you are not alone. In early spring, barred owls are particularly vociferous and often carry on extended conversations well into the night. This is also breeding season and an owl in an amorous mood can produce an impressive array of moans, growls, shrieks, and hoots. The owls should begin as soon as it starts getting dark.

After dark, you'll probably sit around the fire wondering how much longer the wood is going to last. Eventually you retire to your sleeping bag to get a nice restful sleep in the floodplain wilderness. About this time you notice soft rustling sounds interspersed with low growls coming from just beyond the furthest reaches of your flashlight. They grow louder. Being a curious sort and telling yourself you're not afraid, you jump out of your sleeping bag, armed with your Swiss army knife, and creep over to the riverbank. Scanning the shores the flashlight beam picks up reflections of beady red eyes staring back at you. A family of racoons is searching the shores for crayfish and freshwater mussels. Suddenly, a loud splash comes from the river channel just downstream from the racoons. Your flashlight beam focuses on the ripples created by the beaver's tail. Alarmed, he's clearly warning other beavers within earshot of your presence. Later the next morning, you'll see where he came ashore and munched on the bark of several sweetgum trees.

Around four-thirty in the morning you're wishing it will hurry up and get light enough so that you can see the familiar outlines of your campsite. Darkness breeds insecurity. There is a chill in the predawn air and a heavy dew is forming on the grass. The barred owls have finally quieted down and there is not much noise except for the occasional chirp of an awakening bird. Toward the eastern horizon you can see the first hint of the approaching dawn. Thinking of a cup of hot coffee and a warm sweater, you are contemplating getting out of the sleeping bag when suddenly a noise jolts you straight up. Before you have a chance to recover, a second burst echoes from somewhere across the river. You are smack-dab in the middle of two turkey gobblers exchanging their age-old message. The reply and retort session continues through the forest and you sit and listen in awe. The dawn light begins filtering through the crowns of the sugarberries, sycamores, and sweetgums, reaching the forest floor and awakening the other avian inhabitants of the bottomland forest. Cardinals begin their cheerful song, titmice and chickadees begin their chatter, and woodpeckers commence their drum rolls welcoming the new day.

You get up and dress. Immersed in the dawn chorus and energized by the exhilaration of the experience, you quietly walk in the direction of the closest gobbler. Along the way you come to a small clearing. In the gathering light, the forms of twenty-seven browsing deer appear along the far edge, oblivious to your presence. As you approach the edge of the clearing, two pileated woodpeckers, their fiery red crests gleaming in the early morning light, fly across your path, dodging artfully through the trees. You look across the clearing at a grove of cherrybark oaks, their shadow revealing the obscure form of some large morning creature. Raising the binoculars, you see the big gobbler, his body fluffed out to twice its normal size, the beard dangling from his chest nearly to the ground and his fanned-out tail. He puts on a splendid show for the nearby hen. She doesn't seemed to be impressed.

You realize that you're the privileged spectator at one of nature's classic wilderness scenes along the Roanoke. It is a scene enacted daily in the river floodplain where over 50,000 acres of bottomland hardwood forest has been permanently protected in conservation ownership. It is a scene that we should not take for granted. Bottomland hardwoods are threatened by habitat destruction elsewhere on the Roanoke. And, the natural flooding regime to which all of the ecosystem's plants and animals have adapted has been altered by the upstream dams. Currently, efforts are underway by The Nature Conservancy, the U.S. Fish and Wildlife Service, the North Carolina Wildlife Resources Commission, and other conservation organizations and government agencies to restore the flooding regime to approximate the natural cycles of its pre-dam condition. Efforts are also underway to protect another 25,000 acres of bottomland forest so that anyone and everyone who desires to have a wilderness experience will have the ability to do so. Maybe some day visitors to this incredible area will have the opportunity to witness species such as the red wolf and the eastern cougar that once roamed these forest but were exterminated a century ago. Perhaps with enough generosity of spirit and commitment to restoring our native landscape, this ecosystem will fully regain its biotic integrity.

In the meantime, enjoy this watery wonderland, reflect on the overnight camping experience and plan your next trip to the Roanoke, but this time with a friend. The Roanoke has snared another lifelong victim.

J. MERRILL LYNCH

"For those who have learned
to hear its song, the earth can
soothe the troubled heart,
refresh the weary, soften the
hardened, redirect the lost."
Unknown

"Vision Quest"

The vision quest ceremony is a Native American ritual, where the person
seeking a vision goes off into the wilderness alone in search of their purpose in life.
What began as a project to photograph the Roanoke River Basin became
a personal journey of self-discovery. A journey where I learned
to enjoy the simple beauty of a very complex natural world, finding
splendor in the most humble of places.
This was my vision!

"The realization of our true
substance and potential is the
purpose of creation.
The realization of Divine love,
the universal consciousness,
is our responsibility to our creator."

Morihei Ueshiba

LAKE GASTON

THE JOURNEY

"One glances up these paths,
embowered by bent trees, as
though the side aisles of a
cathedral, and expects to hear a
choir chanting from their depths."

Henry David Thoreau

THE JOURNEY

As you view the Roanoke for the first time, it will be hard to distinguish it from any of the many rivers that flow through the Southeastern United States. There are no grand vistas or scenic overlooks to impress you. In fact, there are only a handful of access points from which to view the river along the Roanoke's entire 137-mile course in North Carolina.

During the early stages of my project, a friend asked what I was working on. When I told him that I was photographing the Roanoke River Basin, he asked, "Why? There is nothing there." In one sense he was right, yet it is the river's remoteness that makes the Roanoke unique.

The Roanoke has one of the longest unbroken floodplains in the Southeast. The bottomland hardwood forest that lines its banks, and endless tupelo-cypress swamps make this an intriguing, yet forbidding, place. A tangled mass of vegetation creates an impenetrable wall that protects a maze of backwater swamps teeming with life. Once you penetrate its chaotic exterior and venture deep into its swamps, you will find yourself lost in another world. Surrounded by ancient cypress trees, you feel as if you have been transported back in time.

My first trip to the Roanoke was in June 1995. Filled with excitement and anticipation, I launched my canoe on Conaby Creek, south of Plymouth, North Carolina. It was a beautiful day. The sky was filled with giant cumulus clouds, floating across a Carolina-blue background. Paddling slowly downstream, I came upon a sight that I still consider to be the most memorable scene of these last two years while working on the river. Two pileated woodpeckers were hard at work on a giant cypress tree whose base was surrounded by a patch of water-lilies in full bloom. With a beautiful sky as a backdrop, I knew this was the perfect image. I placed my paddle quietly in the canoe and began to set up my equipment. As I was mounting the camera to the tripod my canoe was caught by the current, sending me totally out of control. Every time I tried to line up the shot, the canoe began spinning wildly, doing its best imitation of a pinwheel. Before I could regain my composure, I realized I was floating right through the scene. This proved to be too much for the woodpeckers. With a look of disgust, they flew off deep into the swamp, no doubt to find a spot where they would not be interrupted again.

This set the tone for the whole weekend, and I soon realized that I would not be able to photograph the river from the canoe. My worst fears were confirmed when I received ten rolls of blurry images from the lab.

On my second trip, I decided to photograph the river from the land. It was a much better approach, and I was finally able to make some good images. However, I quickly became frustrated again after finding only a handful of access points from which to photograph the river. The next obstacle I had to overcome was the remoteness of the region.

On September 22nd, I traveled back to the river. The North Carolina Chapter of the Nature Conservancy was holding its annual meeting at Moratoc Park in Williamston. I decided to go a day early so I could photograph the Roanoke River National Wildlife Refuge before the meeting. A cold front had passed through just before I arrived in Williamston, and stalled off the coast. Undaunted by the rain, I tried to venture into the refuge. I soon learned why the first inhabitants of the region called the river Moratoc, which means "River of Death." The river was prone to flash floods. Without warning, the water level would rise, flooding all the low areas along the river. My well thought-out plan was ruined when I found the refuge under water.

On the day of the meeting, I decided to pack my cameras away and concentrate on getting to know some of the people who lived and worked in the area. That afternoon, I went on my scheduled field trip into Devil's Gut Swamp, a Nature Conservancy Preserve located in Martin County. I decided to scout the area on the tour, then go back the next morning to photograph, if the weather was better.

I spent part of my afternoon walking with Katherine Skinner, who is the Executive Director of the North Carolina Chapter of The Nature Conservancy. Katherine told me about the preserve, and advised me not to go into these swamps alone. Many skilled woodsmen had lost their way here. I assured her that I would not take any unnecessary risks.

The next morning, I entered the swamp at sunrise.The rain had stopped, but it was still overcast, causing the swamp to appear much darker than I had remembered. The combination of strong winds and low light levels made it impossible to photograph. I decided to hike to the far end of the swamp and work my way back. My hope was that the wind would calm down and more light would penetrate the thick canopy of the forest later that morning.

The trail was well marked with yellow tape from the field trip on the previous day. I had no fear of getting lost, yet the darkness and Katherine's warnings became very intimidating. My senses were working overtime. Every sound was magnified; the screech of a hawk, the call of an owl, the drumming of a woodpecker and the sound of wind howling through the trees created an atmosphere straight out of a Stephen King novel. I stopped to regain my composure, thinking how foolish I was being. I had been in situations like this a hundred times before.

I became focused again on my work and began photographing. The time passed quickly and I soon found myself in the backswamp where the largest cypress trees were to be found. Even though it was late September the forest remained very thick and green. There were no signs of Fall. The previous two days of rain contributed to the lushness of the preserve, causing it to come alive.

I was working my way back to my truck when I encountered a tree covered with mushrooms. I stopped to take a closer look and decided to make a photograph. I was adjusting my camera and tripod when it happened. Over the roar of the wind a new sound caught my attention. Chills immediately covered my body. I froze and listened. Was it my imagination? Was my mind playing tricks on me again? No! It was really the sound of an organ playing, and within seconds a choir joined in song. It began and ended so quickly, yet it seemed to go on forever. I felt like I was dreaming in slow motion. As the music faded away, I looked at my watch and saw that it was 9:00 AM. I thought, Where could this have come from? I was in the middle of this primordial swamp. Where was the nearest church? Had anyone else heard this or was it just meant for my ears?

Overwhelmed with emotion, I stood in awe of the giant cypress. I felt so insignificant. It was at that time that I realized I was standing in the center of one of the grandest Cathedrals on this earth. Not a cathedral made by the hand of man, but made by the hand of his Creator. That it was given to us as a gift, not to have dominion over but to be stewards of the land and treat it with the love and respect such a precious gift deserves.

Since that day, my work has gone much smoother. The obstacles that stood in my path seemed to vanish. I made many new friends who helped open doors to some of the private lands along the river and shared with me some of their favorite places. My original plans were to make a photographic book documenting the plants and wildlife of the Roanoke River Basin. The experience I had that Sunday morning in the middle of a Martin County swamp changed the course and purpose of this book.

That morning, I traveled down Moratoc, "The River of Death," and journeyed deep into "The Devil's Gut" to find my life changed forever. I had received my Vision!

May rains
even a nameless stream
is a frightening thing.

Buson

RAINBOW BEND

No Parking

LONG VIEW

BACKSWAMP 1

QUITSNA LANDING

CONABY CROSSING

Sweetwater from 64

ON THE WAY TO SANS SUCCI

Spring wind
the river bank goes on and on
and home is still far away.

Buson

DEVIL'S GUT SWAMP

THE DISCOVERY

"If you want inner peace
find it in solitude, not speed,
and if you find yourself,
look to the land from which you
came and to which you go"

Stewart L. Udall

THE DISCOVERY

Like that first day on Conaby Creek, we often feel that our lives are spinning totally out of control. We find ourselves at the mercy of the wind and current with no way of regaining a steady course. The Roanoke forced me to slow my pace. Once I became in tune with the natural rhythms of the river, I found my work going much smoother. I was no longer fighting the current, but letting it work for me, and when I learned to go with the flow of the river, I regained control of the project.

As I slowed down, and learned to take my time, I began to see the Roanoke in a new way. I was no longer looking out to the horizon in search of beautiful images; instead, I found them close at hand, often right in front of my eyes. With my new sight, I began to find exceptional beauty in some very common places.

During the early stages of my project I would drive from one place to another searching for the perfect scene. I never took the time to really learn any area of the river. It wasn't until I quit rushing around, that I truly began to see and appreciate the subtle beauty of the Roanoke River Basin.

One April morning, I stayed in bed a little longer than planned. It was raining, so there was no point in hurrying out to photograph. Once I did get my gear packed, I headed to the river, pausing at a local restaurant long enough to get some coffee. When I left, I noticed that the rain had stopped and the sky was clearing. An unbelievable sunrise was unfolding. I was nowhere near a suitable place to photograph, so I stopped at the first spot I came to near Quitsna Landing. I parked my truck, put down the tailgate, grabbed my coffee and enjoyed the magical moment. A year earlier I would have scrambled around trying to find a good vantage point, and would have missed the entire experience. I was now able to relax and let go, even though I did not make a single picture that morning. As I sat in the back of my truck, I felt more alive than ever before. Not only did I view this beautiful sunrise, but I experienced it with my whole being. I was able to hear the forest come to life with the rising sun. I felt the warmth of the sun's rays, and was filled with the smell of the swamp's never-ending life cycle. I longed to capture this on film, so those who view my images would be able to see, hear, and feel all that I was experiencing. If I could accomplish this with my photographs, I would have achieved my goal.

The river taught me how to relax. It became my therapy, a place I could go to escape the pressures of daily life and recharge my batteries. I learned how to enjoy life's simple pleasures again, and realized that things did not have to be so complicated.

Most of us live our lives at a very hectic pace. From the time our day starts, we are constantly on the run. From home, to daycare, to work, then back again, we spend our time rushing around, slaves to our own schedules. If we are lucky we may have one evening free of meetings, soccer practice, or activities that keep us constantly busy. We run until we are physically and mentally exhausted, in search of what we consider the good life and then wonder why our lives seem so empty and meaningless. At the end of our day, we relax in front of a television, curl up with a magazine, or surf the net on our computers where we are bombarded with glitzy advertisements and fast-paced commercials that redefine our concept of beauty, while telling us how our lives should be lived. We have become a visually-oriented society whose perception of beauty is being defined by the latest trend and commercialism. Simplicity has been lost!

My journey down the Roanoke was a trip back in time, to a primordial place where I could lose myself in the backswamps and free my mind of all worries. It was a trip to a place where watches and appointment books were not necessary for survival, where I could be nurtured by the healing effects of my natural surroundings, and enjoy the many wonders of the river basin that I was able to see through newly-opened eyes. It was a journey to a place that has remained relatively unchanged, and should remain that way so all can enjoy its healing powers.

RENEWAL

Morningstar

CONINE SPRING

Crescent moon
bent to the shape
of the cold.

Issa

October 19, 1997

Who cares what I think.
I'm no philosopher, I'm not
an authority on anything, yet
I am driven by this passion - this
love of the land - to make these images.
Will they touch anyone? I don't know!
The only thing that I do know is that they have touched me.

SWEETWATER 2

ILLUSION

REFLECTIONS IN LOST POND

LEAVES UNDER ICE 1

Low Water in Backswamp

LEAVES UNDER ICE 3

May 5, 1996

Many of us go through life blind,
until we learn to see with our hearts.

Conine

LEAVES UNDER ICE 2

LEAF COLLECTION

A Touch of Fall

May 30, 1998

*I walk these swamps in search of the hidden
beauty found here, with the hope of creating
a work of art. What I find beneath the bark
of a cypress knee are the carvings of a worm,
or some insect.*

Who is the artist here?

VISION QUEST

THE GIFT

THE FUTURE

"THE DIFFERENCE BETWEEN
LANDSCAPE AND LANDSCAPE
IS SMALL, BUT THERE IS
GREAT DIFFERENCE
IN THE BEHOLDERS"

RALPH WALDO EMERSON

THE FUTURE

The future of the Roanoke for now looks very bright. Many organizations have come together working for a common cause. The Nature Conservancy is continuing its work of preserving land in the region. It has formed an unprecedented partnership with Georgia Pacific to manage and study the Lower Roanoke. They are working hand-in-hand with scientists and naturalists from The North Carolina Wildlife Resources Commission and the Roanoke River National Wildlife Refuge to study and protect this area so all may enjoy its natural beauty.

The Conservation Fund is also active in the region. It has helped form the Roanoke River Partners, which is made up of the five counties that border the river. Their purpose is to promote the region for Heritage and Ecotourism.

By working together, these groups have already begun to make improvements. They are working on building 10 camping platforms in the backwaters that canoeists can paddle to and camp overnight. They have considered the possibility of building a boardwalk and observation deck on Conine Island. There are also plans to build an interpretive center near Windsor, with the help of the Partnership for the Sounds, an organization with similar goals. As new businesses open and these plans become a reality, the region will experience some growing pains.

The Roanoke River Basin has remained relatively untouched because of its remoteness. New highway construction will make the region more accessible in the near future. Currently the Rt. 64 bypass is being built, and when completed, it will provide a four-lane highway to the Williamston area. Another reason the river basin has remained intact is that much of the land is privately owned and being used for farming. At the present time, farming is still profitable, but as the area grows in popularity, the possibility exists that the next generation of landowner could consider selling the land for development.

Many people enjoy spending their leisure time in wilderness areas. With improved roads and an increased awareness of the local charm, the area will begin to experience some of the same problems other popular natural areas across the state have had.

In the mountains of North Carolina, land along the New River that was used for farming is being sold for development. Land along the river that was once used by canoeists and fishermen is now off limits, sometimes causing harsh feelings between those who have used the river for years and the new landowners. Also in the mountains, new laws had to be enacted to protect scenic views along the Blue Ridge Parkway from overdevelopment.

Man is attracted to places of natural beauty, but once he moves there, he immediately begins to make changes to improve the area so it provides him with all the comforts of home. Man unwittingly has a knack for destroying the very thing that attracted him in the first place.

Many believe that this kind of growth will never happen to the Roanoke because of its swampy terrain and a lack of a booming economy. However, all you have to do is take a comparative look at South Florida. If you were gullible enough to purchase some swampland in Florida 25 years ago, it would probably be worth millions today. Its rapid growth has had a serious effect on the environment and the Everglades fragile ecosystem. Habitat vital to a healthy Everglades is being destroyed daily. Restoration work has started to right the mistakes of the past. President Clinton's current budget proposal calls for $331 million in fiscal 1998 to help pay for this work. The American taxpayer is constantly being asked to pay for the mistakes of those who have directly profited from the destruction, while those who have created the problems pay little or nothing toward restoration.

A recent Associated Press article states that Nevada is now the fastest-growing state. Most of Nevada's newcomers settled in the Las Vegas area because of the construction jobs. Currently more than 29,000 new hotel rooms are under construction. Last year 58,000 people moved to Las Vegas. No letup in growth is expected through the year 2000. Water is what limits the desert city's growth, and officials say they have enough water sources to cover the needs until the year 2010. After that, the area faces growth restrictions if no new resources are found.

You may wonder what the rapid growth of Florida and Nevada has to do with the Roanoke River. The reality is that a coastal city in another state is already having an impact on the river.

For over 15 years the state of North Carolina has been in a legal battle with Virginia Beach, Virginia, over a proposed water pipeline from Lake Gaston on the North Carolina-Virginia border. Rapid growth in Virginia Beach has created a water shortage problem. The solution for this problem is to build an 87-mile pipeline from Lake Gaston to Virginia Beach and pump 60 million gallons a day from the Roanoke.

It is not my intention to take sides on this issue, but to raise the question, could things have been done differently? When has a city grown enough? Is it wise for a city to continue to grow when it knows it has a serious water shortage problem? And can this type of growth ever happen along the Lower Roanoke? In the end, the taxpayer pays the price for poor judgment and mismanagement.

The city of Portland, Oregon, stands as a model of what good planning and prudent management can mean to a city. In the late 1970s, it established strict growth restrictions to protect the environment and the city's beautiful setting. Many critics said this would hurt the city's future, but they have been proved wrong. Today Portland is a thriving, prosperous city.

The Roanoke River Basin can also be a model for the future, a place where a corporation like Georgia Pacific works hand-in-hand with a conservation organization like The Nature Conservancy. It can be a place where sensible economic growth can happen without endangering the environment. A place where conservation takes priority over corporate profits and the bottom line. The Roanoke can be a place where a person can escape the pressures of daily life. Whether you are a birder or a hunter, a fisherman or a boater, a weekend photographer or an executive, the Roanoke offers something for us all.

We must all work together to preserve this beautiful wilderness for future generations to enjoy. As The Nature Conservancy states, The Roanoke River is truly "One of the Last Great Places" on this Earth.

BATCHELOR BAY

WILLOW BEND

June 9, 1998

As this project nears completion, so many doubts,
so many unanswered questions.
What next?
Is this book truly my purpose in life,
or has this project merely given my life purpose?
Is there a difference?

ROANOKE RIVER WETLANDS

GREAT ISLAND

CONABY CREEK

CONABY IN FALL

INDIAN WOODS BACKSWAMP

Autumn evening
there's joy also
    in loneliness.

Buson

From Poplar Point Road

July 4, 1998

*How do we maintain our spiritual
connection to the land as technology takes
us further away from it ?*

ALBEMARLE

March 29, 1998

Even if this book is a failure, I have
been given so much by the process.
I have learned the secret to a happy life is
a sharp mind, strong body, and soft heart.
The river has given me all these.

WILLIAMSTON

CONOHO 98

UPPER SWEETWATER

CASHIE

BEHIND LARY'S

MACKY'S LANDING

BELOW QUITSNA

JOURNEY'S END

APPENDIX

"WE DO NOT CHART AND MEASURE THE
VAST FIELD OF NATURE OR EXPRESS HER
WONDERS IN THE TERMS OF SCIENCE;
ON THE CONTRARY WE SEE MIRACLES
ON EVERY HAND....THE MIRACLE OF LIFE
IN SEED AND EGG, THE MIRACLE OF
DEATH IN A LIGHTNING FLASH AND IN
THE SWELLING DEEP."

OHIYESA
(CHARLES ALEXANDER EASTMAN)

Last Stop

July 4, 1998

I launched my canoe from Quitsna landing this morning to float the river one last time. As this journey comes to an end I feel a sense of completion and sadness. The Roanoke has become my home away from home, my sanctuary.

Now I sit on a sandbar, in a bend along the river, reflecting on the last three years. So much has happened, so much has changed. As I look across the river I can see an old abandoned school bus once used by loggers who worked these swamps. How out of place the bus looks, deposited on the river bank with no road to be found. I can only imagine its history. This bus, the only sign of man's presence for miles, makes me wonder what changes are in store for this river, my river.

Twenty years from now, will my daughters and their children find the Roanoke as beautiful and unspoiled as I have found the river basin? Will the Roanoke still have one of the longest unbroken bottomland hardwood forest in the Southeast, or will development and man's so-called progress change the landscape forever? I fear I know the answer.

Many will simply see this piece of work as another book of pretty pictures about nature. These images were meant to challenge. A challenge to begin viewing the natural world differently. The beauty that I found along the banks of the Roanoke can be found as close as our own back yards if we choose to open our eyes.

The Roanoke is every river, every stream, every wetland. The spirit of the Roanoke can be found in every living thing.

July 5, 1998

I have been drawn to Quitsna again. I do not understand the attraction to this location, but I can not recall a trip to the river when I have not visited here. Some of the beautiful images chosen for this book were made from this spot.

Quitsna was once the location of the Tuscarora reservation before our government moved the nation to New York. This area is sacred ground for many, and for others it is simply the end of the road. A place to launch their boats, go fishing, and dump their trash. I have found this spot to be both uplifting and disturbing. Fortunately the Roanoke basin is rather remote, so the littering problem that I found here has not been repeated many times.

As I traveled these waters my thoughts were often with my four daughters. They have been a big part of my life. I have had the opportunity to bring all but one to visit my river. Some day I will share the Roanoke with her. While thinking of them a Rwandan proverb came to mind, it simply states: "We have not inherited the land from our parents, but have borrowed it from our children." I often feel we have squandered our children's inheritance, some through ignorance, some through arrogance. I believe we must begin to look at the land differently. To view it as children do, with wonder and excitement.

This past year I was asked to be the chairperson for the PTA's annual art program at my daughters' elementary school. The Reflection Program is an annual arts competition sponsored by the national PTA. This year's theme was " Wouldn't It Be Great If." One of our students, a fourth grader, won third place in literature at the county level. I found Nick's poem to be very moving.

I will end my journey, not with my thoughts, but with the wisdom of a child, and images of the land we have borrowed from our children!

Wouldn't It Be Great If

Plastic here ... paper there...
we leave trash everywhere.
Pollution is the human game,
I can't believe we're not ashamed.

Wouldn't it be great if
on one special date,
maybe Easter morn or Christmas day
man would suddenly
change his way.

The rivers would flow;
the creeks would run;
there would be a new beginning
for everyone.

No more gas, smoke, water pollution,
no more noise and confusion,
we can have cleaner days
if man changes his destructive ways.

Nick Greco © 1998
Fourth Grade
Piney Grove Elementary School
Kernersville, NC

SACRED GROUND

"CONTINUE TO CONTAMINATE YOUR BED,
AND YOU WILL ONE NIGHT
SUFFOCATE IN YOUR OWN WASTE."

CHIEF SEATTLE 1854

SACRED GROUND I

SACRED GROUND II

END OF THE ROAD

For my four daughters.
May they overlook my many faults,
and inherit the only true thing
of value I own.
My heart.